LIFEBOAT

by Nicola McCartney

LIFEBOAT was first produced by the Catherine Wheels Theatre Company on 6th May 2002, Brunton Theatre Musselburgh, The performance was directed by Gill Robertson, Composer, David Trouton, Lighting Designer, Jeanine Davies, Designer, Karen Tennent, Costume Designer, Karen Tennent. The cast was as follows:

BESS WALDER . . . . Suzanne Robertson

BETH CUMMINGS . . . . Gemma Burns

CHARACTERS

BESS WALDER – from London, 15 years old
BETH CUMMINGS – from Liverpool, 14 years old
Various other parts played by the cast

SETTING

An upturned lifeboat in the North Atlantic

TIME

September 1940.

AUTHOR'S NOTES

In 2001, Gill Robertson, Artistic Director of Catherine Wheels Theatre Company, one of Europe's leading children's theatre companies, read an article in a newspaper about the sinking of the City of Benares, one of the biggest tragedies involving children of the Second World War. The article was an interview with Bess Cummings (née Walder) who was one of the last survivors of the sinking of the SS City of Benares, which was torpedoed by a U-Boat in 1940 with 400 passengers and crew onboard, including 90 children. She had set sail with her younger brother, Louis, and other child evacuees from cities all over war-torn Britain to safety in Canada as part of a Children's Overseas Reception Board mission. After being commissioned to write the script, Gill and I visited Bess at her home in Bishops Cleeve, Gloucestershire and spent a few days with her recording her extraordinary story. This was, for me, the beginning of a friendship with the formidable yet inspirational Bess, for which I am hugely grateful. This friendship lasted until her death in 2010. You can read all about Bess's life online in several obituaries and on The Imperial War Museum website.

Lifeboat, at this point in time, has been performed over 600 times across the world in its award-winning original production by Catherine Wheels, but also in a range of languages and other productions globally. Bess intended her story, and this play, to be an inspiration to young people of the power of friendship, of family, and of, simply hanging on even in the darkest of times.

Nicola McCartney, 2021

Dedicated to the memory of Bess Cummings (nee Walder) 1924-2010, her friend, Beth Cummings, and to the memory of all those children who died when The City of Benares sunk in September 1940.

1.

*Night. The Lifeboat. The sea is rough and stormy. Both
girls cling to the keel of the upturned lifeboat.* **BETH** *is
injured and starts moaning.*

BESS AND BETH There's no place like home. There's no place
like home. There's no place like home...

BESS Mustn't let go. Mustn't. Need to tell... mustn't... I need
to get home. Need to tell them what happened... Hang on.

BETH Who's there?

BESS What happened...? We were asleep, in our cabins, safe
and sound.

I was dreaming... about Canada... about Hollywood... about...
Bang!

BETH A torpoedo... "Abandon ship!"

BESS Abandon ship! Running – run!

BETH Walk! Don't run...

BESS ...To the lifeboats and...

BETH A man. A Sinbad the Sailor man, picked me up and
threw me into a boat. Me and some other children, beside
Mrs Jewelled Hands and Mr Dinner Jacket and two Sinbad
the Sailors.

BESS I was looking all over. I couldn't find him. My brother,
where's my brother? I couldn't see.

BETH Down down down too fast we're going too...

BESS Where's Lou? I lost Lou...

BETH The boat goes splash! Slop slop waves are slopping over the side of the lifeboat.

BESS Slopping onto my feet.

BETH My feet are wet.

BESS The lifeboat is filling up with water.

BETH We're sinking...

BESS We're not supposed to sink. We're supposed to be safe in the lifeboat.

BETH A huge wave picks us up, picks the lifeboat up up up and turns us upside down.

BESS Now.

BETH Now. We're hanging on.

BESS Hanging on to the downside of the lifeboat.

BETH I'm cold, wet...

BESS Scared.

BETH Freezing.

BESS Not scared... got to be brave. Got to tell mum and dad what happened to my little brother Lou.

BETH Bess!

BESS I said I'd look after him... I promised

BETH Bess... Bess Walder?

BESS Beth? Beth Cummings?

BETH Yes... Don't talk Bess. You're hurt.

BESS I need to tell them what happened.

BETH No. You need to hang on. We're going to be rescued. Look, Bess – a rope. Hang onto the rope.

BESS Yes.

BETH We will be rescued. Won't we Bess...? Bess?

BESS Of course we will. The Navy will rescue us. The ships are on their way. Hang on.

BETH We'll hang on.

BESS Yes... Got to tell. Tell Mum and Dad.

BETH Tell Mum.

BESS What happened.

BETH What happened.

BESS The Germans.

BETH The Jerries got us. Sunk our beautiful ship.

BESS They got Lou.

BETH There's no place like home.

BESS There's no place like home.

BETH AND BESS *(together)* There's no place like home...

Music plays on the radio.

---

* A licence to produce LIFEBOAT does not include a performance licence for any third-party or copyrighted music. Licensees should create an original composition or use music in the public domain. For further information, please see Music Use Note on page iii.

2.

Home 1939.

BETH Nineteen thirty nine – four months before the Second World War will start.

BESS Home. My home. Number forty four Rhyl Street, Kentish Town, London.

BETH Home. My home. Orrell Park, the City of Liverpool.

BESS It's a high, high, high, high house. Up the stairs – up past the parlour where Dad's not-allowed-to-touch radio is – past the inside-not-outside bathroom past mine, my very own room, my Lou's-not-allowed-to-touch room because I'm fourteen and I'm the eldest.

BETH And since I'm thirteen and the youngest, I have to share a room with Mum. A lot of people live in my house. There's my Grandma and Grandad, my big brother Geoff who's kind of the leader of the gang and my brother Doug.

BESS I go up and up right to the top... You can see for miles and miles... You can see all over London... I sit up here and wait for the postman. One day that letter's gonna come, "Dear Miss Walder, the Warner Brothers are proud to invite you to appear in their new motion picture..."

DAD Bess! Bess!

BESS My Dad...

BETH Come downstairs this minute!

BESS Dad says I'm "melodramatic" – that means I always exaggerate. But I love my Dad. He lost his finger when a German shot it off in the First World War. He's very brave. Sometimes he sings us songs from the war, from when he was a solider – they're a bit rude!

BESS *joins in with the song.*

DAD *(sings to the tune of What a Friend We have in Jesus)*
WHEN THIS LOUSY WAR IS OVER NO MORE SOLDIERING FOR
    ME,
WHEN I GET MY CIVVY CLOTHES ON, OH HOW HAPPY I SHALL
    BE.
NO MORE CHURCH PARADES ON SUNDAY, NO MORE BEGGING
    FOR A PASS.
YOU CAN TELL THE SERGEANT-MAJOR TO STICK HIS PASSES
    UP HIS ...

BESS *stops* **DAD**.

BESS *joins in.*
PACK UP YOUR TROUBLES IN YOUR OLD KIT BAG AND SMILE
    SMILE SMILE
IF YOU'VE A LUCIFER TO LIGHT YOUR FAG
SMILE BOYS THAT'S THE STYLE!
WHAT'S THE USE OF WORRYING
IT NEVER WAS WORTHWHILE
SO!
PACK UP YOUR TROUBLES IN YOUR OLD KIT BAG
AND SMILE SMILE SMILE!

BESS My Dad is a lot of fun.

BETH Yes he is. I don't have a Dad. He died when I was four.

BESS I'm sorry.

BETH But my Mum is lots of fun. She's my best friend my mum.

BETH'S MUM Right, girl. Get your coat on.

BETH Where are we going Mum?

BETH'S MUM Pictures.

BETH Yes!

BETH'S MUM Just you and me, eh?

BETH *and her* **MUM** *skip like Dorothy towards the cinema.*

BETH I love being alone with Mum because most times she's working or looking after Gran and Grandad and all her brothers and sisters. My mum works hard. She says:

BETH'S MUM You're not going to suffer just cos you've got no father. I'll see to that. Want an ice cream, darling?

BESS Yes please. I love my mum... The film is... amazing... It starts all grey and black and white – Dorothy – that's the hero – goes to save her little dog from the wicked schoolteacher.

BETH'S MUM Beth. Where's your hankie? You've got ice cream all around your mouth.

BETH I forgot it.

BETH'S MUM A real lady, should always carry a handkerchief.

BETH Yes Mum.

BETH'S MUM A real lady, should always carry her lipstick in her handbag... Hey, maybe we'll get fish and chips on the way home, eh?

BETH And then a big twister of a storm picks up her house and spins it way up in to the air with her inside it and it lands in the merry old land of Oz.

BETH'S MUM Sssh!

BETH And suddenly the film goes all technicolor... And Dorothy's walking through the scary forest with her friends, the Tin Man and the Scarecrow... lions and tigers and bears, oh my!

BETH'S MUM Beth, it's starting.

BETH Sorry, Mum... *(whispers)* And I'm skipping a bit, but then she gets these ruby slippers and has to click the heels together three times and say "There's no place like home."

Dorothy, the heroine is played by Judy Garland – boy, can she sing. I want to be a singer one day.

BESS I want to be an actress one day. And one day – one day I'll be in a technicolour movie. One day... And I can tell you something, I'm a far better actress than Judy Garland...

DAD Bess! Lou! Now, I've got a challenge for you two today. To make you more independent. Bess, you listening?

BESS Yes, Dad.

DAD You see where we are – Piccadilly Circus? You saw the way we got here. Now I want you to find your own way home. Lou, you behave yourself... Bess, I want you to look after that young man.

BESS Yes, Dad.

Are you sure you'll be all right?

BESS Of course, Dad.

DAD Good girl You're an adventurer, Bess!

BESS I'm an adventurer... I've travelled through London single-handed and now – the world! I want to go to Canada. My teacher says there are prairies and lakes and mountains and horses in Canada –

A song in the style of Bing Crosby and the Andrews Sisters' **["DON'T FENCE ME IN"]** *plays.**

I want to gallop along the prairie on a big black stallion. *(Writes)* Dear Canadian Travel and Tourism Department, Piccadilly Circus, London.

Bess's mum starts hanging out the laundry.

MUM What are you doing, darling?

---

* A licence to produce LIFEBOAT does not include a performance licence for "DON'T FENCE ME IN". The publisher and author suggest that the licensee contact PRS to ascertain the music publisher and contact such music publisher to license or acquire permission for performance of the song. If a licence or permission is unattainable for "DON'T FENCE ME IN", the licensee may not use the song in LIFEBOAT but should create an original composition in a similar style or use a similar song in the public domain. For further information, please see Music Use Note on page iii.

BESS Nothing, Mum... My mum. The thing about my mum is, she always knows if you're telling fibs... *(To* **MUM***)* Writing a letter.

MUM To who?

BESS I'm going to Canada.

MUM Really? How will you get there?

BESS By ship, of course.

MUM And leave me and dad and Louis behind?

BESS It's just a holiday.

MUM No one goes that far away just for a holiday.

BESS Well, I am. I'm going to get a job singing. In a night club. In London. And I'll save up the money I earn and buy my ticket.

MUM You have it all worked out haven't you?

BESS It's a good plan, isn't it, Mum?

MUM Yes, I suppose it is. Only one problem, though.

BESS What?

MUM You're staying in school! Goodness me, Bess you are a dreamer.

BESS I'm not a dreamer. I will get to Canada – one day, I will!

BETH I'm not a dreamer. I don't want to go anywhere. I want to stay right here with my mum and my two big brothers Geoff and Doug. My brother Geoff is the oldest. He's very handsome.

GEOFF Hey, kid.

BETH Hey Geoff... All the girls fancy Geoff. He is the leader of the gang. Him and his mates all have bicycles and they cycle all over the country.

GEOFF Hey, Kid. You going down the shop?

BETH Yeah.

GEOFF Here you are. Get yourself some pop and a bag of crisps, eh?

He flips her a coin.

BETH Thanks Geoff. *(To audience)* My brother Geoff looks after me. He works so he always has plenty of money for pop and crisps. My mum says he'll make a good catch for a woman one day. But my brother Doug, he's—

DOUG jumps out at BETH, pretending to be a ghost.

DOUG Whoo-ooh!

BETH Doug! You scared me half to death!

DOUG Your face! You want to have seen it.

BETH My brother Doug is very annoying!!

BESS switches on the radio – popular music plays.*

BESS Mum and Dad are out. When Mum and Dad go out, I listen to the not-allowed-to-touch-it radio. The top twenty – Al Bowly, Geraldo and his Orchestra, Vera Lynn. I have to listen in secret. My Dad hates popular music... *(Fantasy)* Ladies and Gentlemen... Tonight, live from Carnegie Hall, we are proud to present, the delectable, the delightful...

LOUIS, dressed as a cowboy, and shooting his guns.

LOUIS Yee-hah! *(Coughs)*

BESS Lou – my little brother. He's very annoying. And he's *always* sick.

To LOUIS.

Shut up and go back to bed!

---

* A licence to produce LIFEBOAT does not include a performance licence for any third-party or copyrighted music. Licensees should create an original composition or use music in the public domain. For further information, please see Music Use Note on page iii.

LOUIS Are you talkin' to me, boy?

BESS You're supposed to be resting.

LOUIS "Said, no low down dirty varmint's gonna look at me that way, Boy... Bang!" ...Awhhh! You touched the radio. I'm telling Dad! *(Coughs)*

BESS I'm allowed.

LOUIS No you're not.

BESS Go away!

LOUIS Bossy boots!

BESS Mummy's boy!

LOUIS Well, I'm telling Dad!

BESS *(to LOU)* Well, I'll tell Mum you got out of bed.

LOUIS Well, I'll tell Dad that you slapped me!

BESS I did not!

LOUIS I know... but I'll tell him that you did.

BESS You little...!

LOUIS Leave me alone! I'm sick. *(Coughs)*

> **LOUIS** *has a real coughing fit.*

BESS Lou...? Take deep breaths. Deep like this... See? All better now.

> **LOUIS** *nods. She puts her arm around him.*

My brother Lou is very annoying... but I love him. *(To LOUIS)*

(fantasy) Star of over fifty best-selling movies, voice of over twenty top ten hits... Please welcome, the delectable, the delightful, the sensational Bess Walder!

BESS *sings along to the wireless. But* **BETH** *turns the dial on the wireless – Italian opera plays*. They listen.*

BETH Isn't it sad?

I could listen to it all day... She's saying that she is sad to leave her home, but she had no choice.

BESS Why has she no choice?

BETH Because of the war...

BESS The War. All everyone's talking about is the war.

BESS/ BETH Bedtime!

BESS *puts on her green dressing gown and sits on the stairs.* **BETH** *sits down on her stairs.*

BESS I don't really understand it all, but it goes something like this. In Germany, there's this man called Hitler.

BETH The Germans call him the Führer. He's a bit like our Prime Minister Mr Chamberlain.

BESS Except that Mr Chamberlain doesn't want to invade every single country in Europe and Hitler does. Hitler even wants to invade Britain, Dad says.

BETH I hear my brother and my Grandad talking about the war. My brother Geoff is in the army. If war breaks out he could get called up at any time.

BESS Dad's friends come round. They listen to the news reports on the wireless and talk and talk and... I'm supposed to be in bed...

BETH Geoff says Hitler can't be allowed to win.

BESS Dad says his children won't go to concentration camps.

BETH What's a concentration camp?

---

* A licence to produce LIFEBOAT does not include a performance licence for any third-party or copyrighted music. Licensees should create an original composition or use music in the public domain. For further information, please see Music Use Note on page iii.

BESS I don't know... Come on. Let's go to bed...

BESS/BETH Our Father which art in heaven, Hallowed be thy name, Thy Kingdom come, thy will be done on earth as it is in heaven...

They continue praying.

3.

Night. The Lifeboat.

BESS/BETH For thine is the kingdom, the power and the glory, for ever and ever...

BETH Bess...

BESS Yes?

BETH I'm scared, Bess.

BESS Hang on...

BETH I'm hanging on...

BESS Waves are dark, icy, angry – bang – the boat keeps.

BETH Bang – Rocking me.

BESS Thump – Throwing me upside bump side down.

BETH Need to keep my.

BESS Head out of the water.

BETH It – smack– hurts...

BESS Glasses, must keep hold of my –

BETH Mum... I want my mum.

BESS Can't see anything without my glasses... Look!

BETH Hanging on...

BESS Hanging on... Other hands. Grown up hands hanging on too.

BETH Mr Leather Gloves.

BESS Mrs Jewelled Hands.

BETH Mr Gold Watch.

BESS And Sinbad the Sailor. Leather Gloves is crying – like Beth – crying. But he's a man, a big grown up man...

BETH I'm not crying... I'm... Breathing... out the dark, angry, icy...

BESS I'm never going to see Lou again. He's dead. How will I tell Mum and Dad what happened?

BETH My feet have lost their slippers – my slippers out there floating in the dark, angry, icy, bobbing in among the cups and plates...

BESS And chairs.

BETH And lampshades.

BESS My legs slipping, can't let go...

BETH Wait... The grown up hands are starting to let go.

BESS Where's Leather Gloves gone?

BETH Mr Gold Watch's fingers uncurling – *(ping ping ping)* – Hold on Bess...

BESS Hold on Beth.

BETH There goes Mrs Jewelled Hands.

BESS Ping! Ping! Ping!

BETH Bye bye – jewelled hands are waving to me from the waves – Bye bye ruby, emerald, sapphire, diamond – bye bye...

BESS Giving up – they're all giving up – why?

BETH Just us now. Alone.

BESS Just you and me. And one Sinbad the Sailor... Are we going to drown too?

BETH No! Don't let go Bess

BESS Won't let go... I won't give up... I won't give up.

A sound like a huge sigh. The ship begins to sink.

BETH What's that noise?

BESS Our ship. Our beautiful bomb-banged ship is dying. Going down...

BETH Under the waves. Sinking...

BESS Down...

BETH Look.

The ship's lights all come on at once.

BESS All her lights have come on.

BETH She looks like a big sparkling jewelled hand.

BESS A big glistening Christmas tree.

BETH A big birthday cake with lots of candles –

BESS Bye bye, beautiful ship.

BETH Bye bye...

BESS Slowly swallowed up in one big—

BETH AND BESS Gulp!

Huge groaning sound as the ship sinks. The lights go off. Rush of water.

BETH Dark.

BESS/**BETH** No!

BESS The sea is clawing at me, pulling on my legs, trying to drag me down into the big big hole after the ship.

BETH Quick.

BESS Kick!

BETH We're going to drown.

They kick with all their might.

No!

BESS You have might have my ship, you might have my brother, you might have my pyjamas – you won't get me. I will not cry.

BETH I will not die. This is war.

BESS *(sings)*

WHEN THIS LOUSY WAR IS OVER I'LL BE HOME AND SAFE AT
LAST

YOU CAN TELL OLD ADOLF HITLER TO STICK HIS WAR RIGHT
UP HIS ...

4.

Home – 1939.

The wireless plays.*

The family listen.

VOICE OF CHAMBERLAIN "I am speaking to you from the Cabinet Room at ten Downing Street. This morning the British Ambassador in Berlin handed the German Government a final note stating that, unless we hear from them by eleven o'clock and they are prepared at once to withdraw their troops from Poland, a state of war would exist between us."

BESS It's the Prime Minister, Mr Chamberlain... We're all gathered round – listening – me, mum, dad and Lou.

BETH Sssh!

BESS Everyone has to be quiet when Dad listens to the wireless.

VOICE OF CHAMBERLAIN "I have to tell you now that no such undertaking has been received, and that consequently this country is at war with Germany..."

BETH I'm scared. I've never seen a war before.

BESS I wonder what it's going to be like?

PUBLIC INFORMATION This is a public service announcement. How to put on your Gaaas Maaask... One: Prepare the maask by ensuring all straps are completely loosened – like so. Two: As you look at the blah blah blah blah blah blah-dee-blah. Blah-dee-blah blah blah. Blah-dee-blah-dee-blah. And finally... Finish by tightening the top straps, in the same manner. The mask should fit snug around the face and chin...

BETH Remember: Hitler will send no warning.

---

*A licence to produce LIFEBOAT does not include a performance licence for any third-party or copyrighted recordings. Licensees should create their own.

BESS Always carry your gas mask.

BETH Remember: Careless talk costs lives.

BESS That's right: there could be spies everywhere.

BETH Spies? Lion's and tigers and bears, oh my!

BESS Loose lips sink ships

BETH Your Britain: fight for it now!

BESS It's a woman's war too!

BETH This is our finest hour.

BESS I'm ready to make a sacrifice, to stand firm against Hitler. I'm ready to do something really special, if I have to.

Air raid siren.

They run to the shelter.

I like air raids.

BETH We have to run – run for our lives – to the shelter.

BESS The air raid shelter's underneath the school down our road. It's... packed... bodies everywhere... You all have to jam in together – mums and dads and children and babies and grannies and grandpas and neighbours and dogs and – hey wait! Get that dog out of here...! Sometimes we have to sleep down here all night until the "All Clear" sounds.

BETH The All Clear's when the Jerries have gone back to Boscheland and it's safe to go back home. We have a shelter at the bottom of our garden. I have to share a bed with Mum, which is good because air raids can be scary.

BESS I have to share a bed – it's not a bed really, it's more like a mattress with Lou, which is really annoying... I lie awake and listen to the bombers over London.

Noise of a German plane.

BETH Brrr – Brrr – Brrr! ...Germans!

Noise of a British plane.

BESS Brrrrrrrr... Our boys.

BETH What's nice is that you feel safe... You know it's dangerous but you go to sleep with all the adults around you, talking, whispering, singing... in the dark.

The people in the shelter start singing.[*]

BESS And in the morning when the all clear sounds, I can go out and collect souvenirs – shrapnel.

BETH I've got two bits of German bomber tail fin and six empty bullet cartridges! My mum says:

BETH'S MUM Ladies do not collect bits of old scrap metal... *(inspects the shrapnel.)* Oh, that looks interesting, where did you find that?

BETH Geoff and Doug have been called up to fight. Mum's very sad. It's just me and her now. So I'm never leaving. I'm going to stay right here and keep her...

BETH'S MUM Darling, listen. I think... It's not safe for you here with all the bombings. Your Auntie has written me from Canada. She wants you to go and stay with her there until the war's over.

BETH How on earth am I going to get to Canada, Mum?...How on earth am I going to get there? We can't afford that.

PUBLIC INFORMATION Are you worried about the safety of your children in wartime Britain? Would you feel better off if you knew they were tucked up in bed somewhere safe and sound? The Children's Overseas Reception Board welcomes applications from parents who wish to send their children abroad to the saftey of families living in Australia, New Zealand, South Africa, the United States and Canada.

BESS Mummy, I'm going to Canada.

---

*A licence to produce LIFEBOAT does not include a performance licence for any third-party or copyrighted recordings. Licensees should create their own.

MUM That's all very well, Bess, but how do you propose to get there?

BESS That's easy. All you have to do is write a letter to the government, saying that I'm allowed to go.

MUM What nonsense! Honestly, what have I told you about telling fibs?

BESS Well, I'm going to go to school tomorrow and get the forms from the C.O.R.B. and then you'll see I'm not telling fibs...and I did.

    BESS *gives* **MUM** *the form.*

BETH And my Mum gave me the form.

BESS My Mum looked at the form...

BETH The Children's Overseas Reception Board.

BESS She looked at it and looked at it... Then Mum gave the form to Dad and he looked at it... And looked at it...

BETH I looked at it and looked at it.

BESS Then he gave the form to Mum and she looked at it again...

BETH I don't want to go away from home. But Mum says it's safer.

BESS And then they talked and talked and talked and talked and talked and talked and

MUM Bess, take this letter to school.

BESS We can go?

MUM We'll see.

BESS So, I hand in the form...

BETH And I handed in my form.

BESS And then...

BETH We wait...

BESS And wait...

BETH And wait... And...

Tests!

BESS *(filling in an exam paper)* I.Q. tests for all children who want to go to Canada. The Children's Overseas Reception Board won't take you if you're not a brainbox – okay, that's an exaggeration – you need to be "above average".

BETH Say "ah!"

BESS Ahhh! ...

BETH Medical tests. The Children's Overseas... You know what it means now... They won't take you if you are sick.

BESS Oh dear, Lou is always sick.

DOCTOR So how many days off school have you had in the past year, Louis?

BESS Oh no.

DOCTOR That's a lot of days off. You must have been quite a sick little boy.

BESS Oh no.

DOCTOR Up on the couch. Let's take a look at you.

BESS Oh no... If Lou is too sick and he can't go then... Well, Dad says, if Lou can't go, then I can't go.

DOCTOR Say ahh!

Pause.

Well, he seems fit enough to me. Clean bill of health!

BESS When can we go? When can we go to Canada? I want to go now.

BETH We have to wait for a letter to come.

BESS Another letter...

BETH An official letter, in a brown envelope which comes On Her Majesty's Service.

BESS I said to the postman. When that letter comes, can you please wave it in the air, so that we know what it is? ...Thank you... Then I went up and up and up and up to the very top of our house. And we waited.

BETH And one day...

BESS The letter!

BETH Mum, the letter's here...

BESS Yes!

BETH So I'm really going then?

BESS I gave Mum the letter... *(To* **MUM***)* Can we open it? Can we?

> **BESS** *at home with* **MUM**.

MUM Sit down and eat your breakfast.

BESS Oh Mum... I pour out the tea from the big brown teapot, mum is very, very quiet. She opens the letter.

> **BESS** *pours out tea from the big brown teapot.* **MUM** *opens the letter. Silence.*

MUM What would you say if I said you could go to Canada.

BESS Yes! When can we go? When?

MUM Settle down! Settle... There's a few things we have to organise first. You're going to stay with your Auntie Joyce and Uncle George in Vancouver.

BESS I can't believe I'm really going to Canada! At last! I'm gonna be a movie star!

BESS *(reading the letter)*	**BETH** *(reading the letter)*
Please get your children to Euston Station at nine am on twelfth September nineteen forty – that's next week! – ready to embark for an unknown port... An unknown port...	Please have your children ready to leave at eleven am on twelfth September nineteen for— – that's tomorrow – ready to embark for an unknown port...

BETH Lions and tigers and bears, oh my...!

BESS Now I'm getting my bags packed. A trunk – a big trunk which Dad brings down from the attic. I'm taking all my books and all of my clothes and – oh, yes! – all of my brochures from the Canadian Tourist Board and my...

BETH Excuse me... Please pack for each girl the following items: one dress, one jumper, one change of underclothes, one pair summer shoes, one pair winter shoes, and one luxury item.

BESS I'm taking my green dressing gown, even though it's old and worn. I like it.

BETH Please pack these into a small suitcase... *(Looks at* **BESS***'s trunk)* A small suitcase...

BESS I can't believe it.

BETH I'm really going.

5.

The Lifeboat. Sunrise.

BETH Bess, look at the sun.

BESS It's morning...

BETH We've been hanging on to this lifeboat all night.

BESS Red sky.

BETH Red sky means stormy weather.

BESS Oh no...

BETH Mum will give the government what for when she finds out what the Germans did to us. And my brother Geoff... he'll give 'em what for...

BESS My brother...

Beth... I... Can't hold on much longer.

BETH Have to... for Mum...

It starts to shower down with hailstones.

BESS Getting dark again.

BETH Storm clouds.

BESS Rain.

BETH Sleet.

BESS Hailstones.

BETH Big heavy jaggy hailstones.

BESS Drumming down on us.

BETH Can't feel my fingers.

BESS Can't feel my toes...

BETH Someone must come looking for us soon.

BESS Beth.

BETH They must.

BESS Look! Over there...

Beth.

BETH What...

BESS A right-side up boat coming towards us.

BESS AND BETH Lifeboat.

BESS Try to shout... Hey!

BETH Hey! *(To* **BESS***)* Try to shout...

BESS I want to... wave... but... Can't... Can't let go of the rope.

BETH They're coming to us, Bess. They're coming.

BESS We're going to be rescued.

BETH That's it... Come on... Come on... Come on come on come on...

BESS What's it doing?

BETH It's turning around.

BESS No... No... Come back... Hey! Hey!

BETH Sssh...

Pause. The lifeboat fades out of sight.

BESS Oh no.

BETH Oh no.

6.

Euston Station.

BESS Twelfth September Nineteen Forty. Nine a.m. Euston Station. Everywhere – children – big, small, fat, thin, dark, blonde, dirty, shiny, cheeky, Cockney, posh, noisy, crying, smelly, smiley, everywhere children. And mums and dads. All of them crying...

Italian Opera music plays*. Tableaux of the children leaving their parents at Euston station.

And crying... Still crying... everywhere floods and floods of tears. My Mum and Dad...

MUM Now, listen here, my darling: grow up to be a good girl won't you?

BESS Yes, Mum...

DAD Now, listen here, young woman: I know Louis can be a naughty young man, but I want you to look after him. Promise?

BESS I promise. *(To audience)* And then we hugged and kissed and Dad said:

DAD Okay, time for us to be off.

BESS And they went. Down the platform, arm in arm. Mummy leaning into Daddy. They didn't look back at us...

BETH The woman – the official lady – came to our house at eleven am, sharp. I hugged my mum and kissed her. She was trying hard not to cry... I walked with lady to the end of our street and to the corner.

Silence. She waves. Her **MUM** *waves back.*

---

* A licence to produce LIFEBOAT does not include a performance licence for any third-party or copyrighted music. Licensees should create an original composition or use music in the public domain. For further information, please see Music Use Note on page iii.

MUM Bye bye, darlin. Bye bye.

BETH I was trying hard not to cry... We got on a tram and went into the city centre.

Guard's whistle blows.

BESS We're on the train now. Bang goes the door to our carriage. Children piling in. One by two bang by three slam by twenty. Bang. Suitcases one on top of the other. Bang bang slam. Heads hanging out of windows, kisses, tears, sighs, farewells, fainting... And...

The train pulls out of the station, gathering speed.

BESS/BETH We're off! ...And we're off...and we're off...and we're off...and we're off...

BESS And the crying is – stopping... And we're off to an unknown port... an unknown port an unknown port an unknown port... And as if by magic...unknown, unknown, unknown, unknown, unknown... The children are suddenly smiling... Canada Canada Canada Canada... And singing...

A song in the style of Vera Lynn's [**"WISH ME LUCK AS YOU WAVE ME GOODBYE"**] *plays*.

GUSSIE Vi! Violet! Sit down or I'll box yer ears! Remember what Mum said – I'm in charge! ...Connie, you'll eat what yer bloomin well given to eat and like it! Eddie, Lenny! Stop that!

BESS A girl in my carriage...

---

* A licence to produce LIFEBOAT does not include a performance licence for "WISH ME LUCK AS YOU WAVE ME GOODBYE". The publisher and author suggest that the licensee contact PRS to ascertain the music publisher and contact such music publisher to license or acquire permission for performance of the song. If a licence or permission is unattainable for "WISH ME LUCK AS YOU WAVE ME GOODBYE", the licensee may not use the song in LIFEBOAT but should create an original composition in a similar style or use a similar song in the public domain. For further information, please see Music Use Note on page iii.

GUSSIE All right? I'm Gussie – Augusta really, but that sounds too stuck up. Gussie Grimmond.

BESS Bess. Pleased to meet you.

GUSSIE Violet! I told you to sit down... Kids are a bloomin nuisance, I'm tellin you. You got any sprogs to look after?

BESS Just one – how many have you got?

GUSSIE Four – 'scuse me. *(Slaps a kid)* Told you, leave him alone.

BESS Why are you wearing your nightgown?

GUSSIE Oh that... Got bombed out last night, didn't we? Jerries dropped a bomb right on top of our house. Lost everyfing but the clothes we was standin up – or ravver – lyin dahn in – at the time. My Dad, he says, "That's it! I've just abaht had abloodynuff of this. We're getting you kids the hell out of here." One of those Home Office ladies wiv all he sandwiches says she'll get us new clothes when we get where we're goin. Lenny! Right, you little...

BESS/BETH Canada Canada Canada Canada...

BESS Fields, trees, houses.

BETH Houses, trees, fields.

BESS/BETH Stop...

BESS Our stops? A station? What station? No signs. No names. Where are we?

BETH/BESS And.

We're off!

Fields, trees, houses.

BESS Horses!

BETH/BESS Houses, trees, fields.

BETH Factories.

BESS/BETH Stop!

BETH Everybody out.

Air raid air raid! Under the train…

BESS/BETH …And.

We're off.

Fields, farms, factories.

BESS I'm sleepy.

BETH Getting.

BESS Stop.

Sleepy.

BETH Stop.

BESS Stop.

BETH Stop.

BETH An unknown port.

BESS Liverpool.

BETH Liverpool, the unknown port is Liverpool?!

BESS The lady from the C.O.R.B. says we have to keep everything really secret. Because we're going on a special voyage. Even mums and dads can't know where we are. That's because there are spies everywhere…

BETH Spies… Lions and tigers and bears oh my.

BETH/BESS Lions and tigers and bears oh my.

BESS Then we see it.

BETH The ship

Our ship

BESS She's called, The City of Benares. The most wonderful ship I've ever seen.

BETH The City of Benares… Look at it.

BESS It's…

BETH It's

They board the ship.

An **INDIAN STEWARD** *greets them.*

BESS Open Sesame!

Before us a big man with a silver turban and shoes that turn up at the ends.

INDIAN STEWARD Welcome aboard, little madam.

BESS Crikey! No one's ever called me madam before. Are you called Sinbad – like the Sailor from the Arabian Nights?

INDIAN STEWARD No, little madam... I am Iqbal, your steward.

BESS Golly! It's the biggest, grandest, most fantastic ship I've ever seen.

BETH It's a big, big ship. Much bigger than all the other ships in the docks. *(Looks over the side)*

BESS Line up! Line up, ready for inspection.

BETH A lady, a very tall and very gentle lady called...

MARY CORNISH Careful now. Careful on the gangplank, children.

BETH Miss Mary Cornish – our escort. The escorts are here to look after us. They've volunteered to sail all the way to Canada, just to make sure we get there safely.

MARY CORNISH Girls – you will be in Cabins on the starboard side. Boys, cabins to port... That's left... *(To* **BETH***)* Don't cry, darling. Don't...

BETH I miss my Mum.

MARY CORNISH I know, darling, I know. Come on now. It's an awfully big adventure, see? And we're going to have lots and lots of fun. Now this is your cabin.

BETH My cabin...

BESS My cabin. Bye bye Louis. Behave! ...

BETH I've never seen so much carpet.

BESS I've never seen such beautiful paintings.

BETH I've never seen so much gold and silver.

BESS I've never seen such comfortable beds.

BETH I like my own bed. I miss my mum

BESS Mum said, "Grow up to be a good girl." Why did she say that...? Mum thinks she's never going to see me again.

BETH *(closes her eyes and taps her heels together three times)* There's no place like home...

BESS *(closes her eyes and taps her heels together three times)* There's no place like home...

The girls notice each other.

BETH There's no place like home.

BESS There's no place like home.

BETH Hello.

BESS Hello.

BETH	**BESS**
That's my favourite film.	That's my favourite film.
No. Really? Mine too.	No. Really? Mine too.

They laugh.

BESS I've memorised most of the script.

BETH Really.

BESS Oh, yes. I want to be an actor one day.

BETH Really... I'm going to be a nurse. Or an opera singer. I don't know which at the moment.

BESS My name's Bess.

BETH My name's Beth.

BESS/BETH Pleased to meet you.

They shake hands.

Sound of the ship's horn blasting.

BESS And we're off... Setting sail.

BETH Leaving Liverpool.

BESS The City of Benares... Sailing... Away.

BETH Away from home. On the ship waving, laughing, singing.

BESS/BETH "Wish me luck as you wave me goodbye...".

BESS On the docks... Waving... Shouting... Waving... Singing.

BETH/BESS Bye bye.

Blast on the ship's horn.

BETH The ship is singing.

The other ships in the convoy begin to sound their horns too.

BESS All the other ships are singing too.

BETH/BESS Bye bye.

Bye bye bye.

Goodbye.

7.

On the ship.

BETH Dear Mum,

It is now two days since we set sail. It is very lovely here on the ship. The sun is shining but it's cold on deck. I wish you were with us. We have men from Calcutta to wait on us. They do everything for us – clean our shoes and clean our rooms. They are very kind to us. We have our tea in a big dining room with silver knives and forks – three different kinds of knives and forks. I get a bit confused, but my new friend Bess is showing me how to use them. We can choose what we like off a menu! There's roast beef and ham and chocolate and jelly and ice cream and trifle and all sorts of things...

BESS *claps her hands.*

STEWARD Yes, little madam?

BETH I would like something to eat please.

STEWARD Yes, little madam.

BETH I would like... a bar of chocolate please.

And as if by magic... The **STEWARD** *produces the bar.*

STEWARD One bar of chocolate, little madam.

BESS Thank you...

I would like...

STEWARD Yes, little madam?

BETH I would like a big ham roll, please.

And as if by magic... The **STEWARD** *produces the roll.*

STEWARD One ham roll, little madam. Will that be all?

BETH Yes, thank you.

BESS Crikey!

BETH Golly!

BESS This is the life.

BETH This is the life of a movie star.

BESS Yes... One day, when I'm famous, I'll have a house as big as this ship.

BETH Will it have – a ballroom?

In the ballroom – they dance.

BESS Yes.

BETH Will it have, a swimming pool?

In the swimming pool – they splash about.

BESS Two swimming pools. Come in, the water's lovely.

BETH No thanks... I can't swim.

BESS You can't? Why not? My dad taught me.

BETH My mum wouldn't let me. She says the water's dangerous.

A bell rings.

We have four lifeboat drills everyday. Our officers are all Scottish. A lifeboat drill is when you have to put on your lifejackets and...

OFFICER *(speaks in a Scottish accent)* Walk – don't run!

They put on life jackets and run.

BETH To the muster station.

OFFICER *(speaks in a Scottish accent)* In an orderly fashion please!

BETH That's where you meet.

Our muster station is in the nursery where there's this huge rocking horse. Sometimes me and Bess sneak in there and have a go, even though the rule is we're not allowed.

BESS Come on it'll be an adventure.

The girls enter the nursery and **BESS** *climbs on the rocking horse.*

*A song in the style of Bing Crosby and the Andrews Sisters' [***"DON'T FENCE ME IN"***]* *plays*.*

BETH We do a lot of singing. Every afternoon we have a tea party in the ballroom with Miss Cornish.

*Piano music plays**.*

MARY CORNISH Sing up now: Merseydotesand dozydotes and littlelambsydiveys, a kiddlydiveytoo, wouldn't you?

Music continues.

BETH Miss Cornish is a music teacher. She's very kind and plays the piano for us.

BESS And organises games on deck.

They play deck games.

Port!

They run left.

BETH Starboard!

---

* A licence to produce LIFEBOAT does not include a performance licence for "DON'T FENCE ME IN". The publisher and author suggest that the licensee contact PRS to ascertain the music publisher and contact such music publisher to license or acquire permission for performance of the song. If a licence or permission is unattainable for "DON'T FENCE ME IN", the licensee may not use the song in LIFEBOAT but should create an original composition in a similar style or use a similar song in the public domain. For further information, please see Music Use Note on page iii.

** A licence to produce LIFEBOAT does not include a performance licence for any third-party or copyrighted music. Licensees should create an original composition or use music in the public domain. For further information, please see Music Use Note on page iii.

They run right.

BESS Captain's coming!

They stand to attention. Salute.

BETH Port!

BESS Bombs overhead!

They dive to the floor and cover their heads.

BETH Sometimes Bess and I need to get away from the little ones. We sneak away up on the upper deck on our own.

BESS You're not really supposed to go there.

BETH We wave at the other ships in our convoy.

BESS Look at that officer in his uniform. Isn't he handsome?

BETH Yeah.

BESS I like a man in uniform.

BETH My brother Geoff wears a uniform. He's much more handsome than that.

BESS He's smiling at you.

BETH No he's not.

BESS He is. *(To Sailor)* Hey!

They duck.

BETH Bess!

BESS Look at your face!

BETH You can see the whole ship from up here. All the children running around below... There's a little boy on the boat called Johnny Baker who runs everywhere with his collar turned up pretending to be a horse. He's going to live on a farm on a prairie.

JOHNNY BAKER *does his horse impression.*

BETH And a girl called Sonia Bech who has a beautiful camel-haired coat which she wears all the time.

BESS He banged into me!

BETH Do tell that little boy to stop being so rough.

Sonia's quite posh but she's really nice... And then there's my room mate, Patricia. She's from Liverpool too, so we're great friends. Patricia's been on a ship going to Canada which was torpedoed, just last month. She keeps telling us:

BESS Don't worry! If we get torpedoed the Royal Navy will rescue us. So don't worry.

BETH Don't worry, Mum. Us children all get on well. And our escorts really look after us – not as good as you would, Mum, but almost.

Sound of a child crying.

BESS/BETH Joyce!

BETH There's a little girl called Joyce Keeley from London who keeps crying to go home all the time...

BESS Dear Mum and Dad, We are all very excited about going to Canada.

BETH Don't worry about me, Mum. I'm alright.

BESS We have set sail and I am enjoying myself immensely. I was a bit seasick at first, but have found what they call my sea legs now... There is a lady film-maker on the ship called Ruby Grierson. I can't believe it a real live film director right here under my nose! She's come to make a film of us.

RUBY *enters, wearing a beret and carrying and smoking a long cigarette holder. She is filming.*

RUBY Okay, you guys, just carry on doing what you're doing. Act normal.

BESS She quite nice to us and it's fun to pose for the camera.

RUBY Okay. Like the singing. Good singing. Good. But, I was thinking, Maybe...

BESS The trouble is, she keeps asking us to do silly things.

RUBY Yeah... I've got it. You know what would be really great for the folks back home, would be to see you kids all singing something really really English. Know what I mean? ...You kids, do you know the words to An English Country Garden? Y'know, "How many kinds of sweet flowers grow in an English country garden" ...da da da da, y'know – forget-me-nots and daffodils...?

BESS No.

RUBY No? I thought you kids knew all the songs.

BESS Me and my friend (BETH), we can sing a song for you.

RUBY Oh yeah?

BESS Yeah.

RUBY Go ahead. I got ya.

BESS Swell.

RUBY Swell? This kid talks like she's in a movie!

> BETH *and* BESS *together sing a popular song of the 1940s*[*].

> *A bell rings.*

BETH We've had ten practices of lifeboat drill now in case our boat sinks but don't worry about that Mum because we are sailing in what they call convoy, with all the smaller ships around us.

BESS Don't worry, because we have three ships from the Royal Navy sailing with us all the way to Canada.

---

[*] A licence to produce LIFEBOAT does not include a performance licence for any third-party or copyrighted music. Licensees should create an original composition or use music in the public domain. For further information, please see Music Use Note on page iii.

BETH Me and Bess stand on deck and wave to the other boats...

BESS I am keeping an eye on Louis, although he is on the boys side and I am with the girls.

BETH Don't worry about me Mum.

BESS Don't worry about us.

> *Music of the hymn* [**"ETERNAL FATHER, STRONG TO SAVE"**] *plays.*

BETH We have prayers twice a day. And we have to sing this hymn a lot which I don't like. It's about asking God to save you from all the different ways you can die on the sea.

BETH/BESS *(sing the last few lines)*
... OH HEAR US WHEN WE CRY TO THEE
FOR THOSE IN PERIL ON THE SEA

BETH It scares me.

BESS Don't worry. We'll be all right.

BETH The weather is turning really nasty.

BESS There's a storm brewing.

BETH Like the one that blew Dorothy's house away.

BESS I'll get you my pretty.

> *The ship rocks about more violently. Game of Port and Starboard.*

BETH Port!

BESS Starboard!

BETH At ease! Whooah!

BESS Bombs overhead. Whooah!

BETH/BESS Portstarboard.

BESS/BETH Foreaft.

> **BESS** *is seasick.*

BETH Are you all right...? We'd better get you downstairs.

BESS Hang on.

BETH What for...? What's wrong? Bess?

BESS The Navy... Where have the Navy ships gone?

BETH I don't know.

BESS They said they were coming with us all the way to Canada.

BETH They've.

BESS Vanished.

BETH Grey.

BESS Dark.

BETH Quiet.

BESS Grey everywhere as far as the eye can see.

BETH It's only six o'clock.

BESS All's not well.

BETH It's only six o'clock and they put us to bed, with no tea.

BESS I couldn't eat any tea.

BETH Up the wooden hill to Bedfordshire.

BESS Sleep.

BETH I can't sleep.

BESS Go to sleep.

They sleep.

Sound of a torpedo approaching.

An explosion and the ship rocks violently.

The girls are thrown out of bed. A bell rings.

*Sound of chaos on board; ship creaking, alarm noise
etc. The girls move to reflect the "chaos".*

The wardrobe just missed my legs, but it fell right on top
of Alice. She couldn't move. We tried to lift the wardrobe
but it was too heavy.

BETH My leg was hurt, it was bleeding. I could hardly walk.

BESS Alice was trapped.

We tried to help her. But we were told to go on deck. We
had to leave Alice behind.

The girls put their life jackets on.

The water was up to our ankles. We tried to go up the usual
staircase but it had collapsed. I could see through the floor
– there were big gaps everywhere down down down into
the decks below.

BETH One of the escorts, picked me up because I couldn't walk
and carried me upstairs to the deck.

The girls move through the chaos.

It was pitch black on deck. The only light was from the
fireworks, no not fireworks, flares. The sky was all red and
yellow like on bonfire night. It was really pretty.

BETH	**BESS**
A man lifted me into a lifeboat.	A man lifted me into a lifeboat.

BESS I was looking for Lou.

BETH They started to lower the lifeboat into the sea.

BESS I was looking for my brother.

BETH I was thinking, we're going to be safe now.

BESS Then.

BETH The end of the lifeboat – my end started dipping.

BESS We were going down at an angle, heading into the sea.

BETH I looked up. Above us the ropes were entangled. A sailor took a knife and cut the ropes and we...

BESS Plunged into the ocean...

BETH It was alright...we were floating.

BESS But then.

BETH The lifeboat's filling up with...

BESS Water.

BETH Water? *(In pain)* Salt hurts. My leg hurts.

BESS Water. Up to my knees.

BETH I say to the little children beside me, "Keep your heads up."

BESS Up to my waist...

BETH The little ones are drowning.

BESS Up to my chest...

BETH Up, up, up.

BESS/BETH Keep your heads up.

BESS They're drowning.

  Pause.

BETH Oh no.

BESS Don't think about it.

BETH Don't think

BESS The lifeboat's sinking.

BETH Water up

BESS To my neck.

BETH To my chin.

BESS Deep breath!

  BETH *and* **BESS** *both take a huge breath.*

The lifeboat capsizes.

They are under the water.

Down... Cold and dark and... And... And... Lost my pyjama bottoms... Nearly lost my... Glasses... My glasses... Drowning... No... Not drowning...

BETH Down... Like a lift out of control, like a Big Ferris wheel too fast... I can't swim, what do I do? I can't swim... Too fast...going to hit the... No... Got to...

BESS Remember what Dad said... Remember...

DAD Remember, young woman. Here's the thing about diving. A human being is like a cork – it floats. When you go under... Relax... Let your arms go... Wide... Float... That's it... No point kicking. Save your strength... That's it... When you come up... That's when the work really starts... Now kick...

They swim to the surface and break through.

BESS *and* **BETH** *cling to the lifeboat. The sun rises.*

BESS Beth...?

BETH Mm-hmmm?

BESS I think I might be nearly dead.

BETH Me too.

BESS Should we just let go?

VOICES Hello... Hello... It's children... How many... One, two, maybe three... Hang on we're coming.

BETH Where am I?

BESS It's very quiet.

BETH It's a ship, another ship.

BESS I'm warm.

BETH I'm dry.

BESS What's the ship called?

BETH AND BESS The HMS Hurricane.

BESS *(trying to move)* Lou... I've got to see if he's...

>   BESS *is in too much pain and stops.*

BETH Where's Bess?

BESS I am asking for Lou.

BETH I am asking for Joyce and Gussie and all the little Grimmonds and Patricia from Liverpool.

BESS I am asking for my brother. But... *(A beat)* My brother is dead.

BETH They are dead. All dead.

BESS What will I tell my Mum and Dad?

BETH Even Patricia is dead.

BESS AND BETH But I'm alive...

BESS I want to be alive but...

CAPTAIN Sit up, miss! I have a present for you.

BESS A present?

>   *(to herself)* The only present I want is to go home. Go home and tell mum and dad what happened to...

CAPTAIN Is this you brother, by any chance?

BESS Lou...? The "present" peeps out from behind the Captain's back. I put on my glasses...

>   LOUIS *appears.*

>   It's you! Where on earth have you been?

LOUIS What do you mean where on earth have I been? Where have you been?

BESS I can't believe it.

LOUIS My sister, I told you it was my sister!

BESS *hugs him and kisses him, until* **LOUIS** *has enough.*

Get off! Stop slobbering all over me. I'm not a baby.

BESS How did you know I was here?

LOUIS Easy… I saw your woolly green dressing gown hanging up to dry and I said to the Captain, "That's my sister's, that is."

BESS My dressing gown.

BETH The rescue ship is turning, heading for Scotland. Taking us back to Britain. Taking us home.

BESS There's no place like home.

BETH Bess, we made it.

BESS Yes.

BETH Us and nine other children.

BESS Eleven.

BETH Only eleven of us out of the ninety-eight that set sail from Liverpool.

BESS Johnny Baker, Sonia Bech, Sinbad the Sailor. Where's Miss Cornish?

BETH Over there… She saved the lives of six boys! She told them stories to keep them awake all night and kept them singing.

Music.*

I was fourteen when the ship sank.

BESS I was fifteen.

BETH I'm seventy-eight-years old now.

BESS And I'm seventy nine.

BETH And we're still friends.

---

* A licence to produce LIFEBOAT does not include a performance licence for any third-party or copyrighted music. Licensees should create an original composition or use music in the public domain. For further information, please see Music Use Note on page iii.

BESS All these years and years later.

     Then they took us to Scotland, to hospital.

     And that's where we stayed all through the war.

BETH And then what happened?

BESS Well, after the war, I went back to London.

BETH And I went back to Liverpool. I took singing lessons and sang on stage in an opera.

BESS But you didn't become a singer.

BETH No.

BESS And you didn't become a nurse.

BETH No. I worked – wait for it – a shipping company!

BESS And I became a schoolteacher.

BETH Not an actor, then?

BESS No. Mum was right. I never did get to Canada. I never did get to Hollywood. But I got a husband – Geoff.

BETH My brother Geoff. I introduced you.

BESS That's right. He was very handsome in his uniform and I thought, "I'll have him, please."

BETH And you're happy.

BESS I'm very happy.

BETH I still remember the smell of the rubber flooring in the ship.

BESS I still remember the taste of the ham roll.

BETH I have lots of pictures on my walls of the City of Benares, and the HMS Hurricane.

BESS I have letters and photographs.

BETH And every year we meet up, with the others.

BESS The others who survived. And we remember the ones who didn't.

BETH I still remember.

BESS Ruby Grierson.

BETH Gussie Grimmond.

BESS And Violet and Connie.

BETH And Eddy and Lenny.

BESS/BETH Joyce Keeley!

BESS We still remember.

BETH We didn't let go. Why didn't we let go?

BESS Well, we couldn't give up, could we?

BETH That's right. We were not in the business of giving up.

BESS/BETH We hung on.

End

ABOUT THE AUTHOR

Nicola McCartney is a playwright, director and dramaturg. She trained as a director with Citizen Theatre/G&J Productions and Charabanc Theatre Company, Belfast. Nicola was Artistic Director of Lookout Theatre Company, Glasgow from 1992–2002, and has twice been an Associate Playwright of Playwrights' Studio Scotland. She has worked for a host of organisations as a dramaturg including Vanishing Point and Stellar Quines/Edinburgh International Festival. Her plays include: *Easy, Heritage, Home, Standing Wave: Delia Derbyshire in the 60s, Rachel's House, Cave Dwellers, How Not To Drown* and *Lifeboat*. She is also a social theatre practitioner and has worked with all sorts of groups including people within the criminal justice system in the UK and USA, asylum seekers and refugees, drug users, survivors of domestic violence and childhood abuse. Nicola has worked with Traverse's flagship outreach programme, Class Act, since 1997, taking it to Russia, Ukraine and India. In 2018 she was a recipient of a Writers' Guild of Great Britain Olwen Wymark Award for encouraging theatre in the UK. Nicola is currently Reader in Writing for Performance at the University of Edinburgh where she leads the Masters programme in Playwriting.

How Not To Drown